D0466459

anythink

SUPER CARS

A celebration of iconic marques

Mason Crest

Contents

Mason Crest
450 Parkway Drive, Suite D
Broomall, PA 19008
www.masoncrest.com

Printed and bound in the United States of America.

10 9 8 7 6 5 4 3 2 1

Cataloging-in-Publication Data on file with the Library of Congress.

Series ISBN: 978-1-4222-3275-0
Hardback ISBN: 978-1-4222-3283-5
ebook ISBN: 978-1-4222-8521-3

Written by: Devon Bailey

Images courtesy of Magic Car Pics, Corbis and Shutterstock

Introduction

For decades, car manufacturers have constantly developed innovative ideas that push the boundaries of speed and power in order to fuel the production of incredible supercars. The supercar has experienced an evolutionary journey, with companies exploring the application of race-derived engineering, aerodynamic styling, and hybrid technology. The engineering development of added aesthetic value and impressive track specifications have played a huge role in the automotive market of supercars, both beneath the hood and on the exterior.

In order to qualify as a supercar, a prototype model must: be produced in enough numbers to be classed as a production vehicle, deliver breathtaking speed, demonstrate revolutionary design or technology, and be labeled with an eye-watering price tag. Since the beginning of the supercar era, through the financial boom of the 1980s (that inevitably led to the rise in demand and market sales of supercars), and up to the present-day evolutionary development of eco-friendly hybrid vehicles, the automotive trade has been on the lookout for what innovative moves each manufacturer will make next in order for their name to be at the top of the supercar list.

Many supercar manufacturers spent years developing their engines to make them faster, adapting construction materials to make them lighter, and focusing on obliterating world records for the fastest production vehicle as a means of gaining positive press and shifting units. The world record (for speed) is currently held by the Bugatti Veyron Super Sport (with an officially recorded top speed of 269mph), although it is inevitable that others will develop even faster engines for road-legal production vehicles. In February 2014, the Hennessey Venom GT achieved an impressive 270mph, although this has not yet been given as an official record.

This publication explores a selection of the best supercars to date including the most popular models from Aston Martin, Jaguar, McLaren, Nissan, Bugatti, Porsche, Ferrari, Chevrolet, Dodge, Ford, Mercedes, Gumpert, Noble, Pagani, and more.

Strength, speed, agility, and stunning cosmetic qualities are what define the term "supercar." While supercars are intentionally built for the elitist upper-end of the market, technological developments have allowed certain car manufacturers to lower production costs, even during financially difficult times. As long as you have a very healthy bank account, you can probably afford to buy one of these revolutionary vehicles.

Ariel Atom

The story of the Atom begins in 1996 when Coventry University student Niki Smart started to develop a car with input and funding from British Steel and Tom Walkinshaw Racing (TWR). It made its public debut in 1996 at the British International Motor Show at the Birmingham National Exhibition Centre. Since its conception in 1996, the Atom has experienced a number of evolutionary changes to improve handling, performance, and comfort. Four power outputs are available according to each model with a range from 245 to 500bhp.

Each car is hand built with exceptional care and craftsmanship; the chassis is constructed by expert welders to ensure the highest levels of quality and safety are achieved. With almost non-existent bodywork, the raw energy is proudly on display through the exoskeleton steel frame. It is powered by a Honda 2.0-liter i-VTEC engine, and is available as a normally aspirated or supercharged variant. The supercharged engine boasts 300bhp which, coupled with the Atom's extremely low weight of just 1102lb (500kg), translates to an incredible 600bhp per ton – more than a Ferrari Enzo.

The suspension is derived from a single-seat racing car, and has been tuned by Lotus. Despite its racecar-like handling, it offers a comfortable ride on the road courtesy of the rubber bushings on the adjustable suspension rod ends that absorb road shocks and reduce noise entering the car. Extensive wind tunnel testing allowed the designers to figure out the aerodynamics of the Atom. The underbody is positioned low in order to decrease airflow, while the shape of the body generates downforce to the front and rear of the vehicle, increasing traction and enhancing handling characteristics. Behind the wheel the driver sits on a molded composite seat and is faced with a race-derived LED screen displaying revs, speed, and temperature.

The Atom may lack a number of mod cons such as a heater and a stereo (in fact it doesn't even have a roof, doors, or windscreen)

Production	1996 to present
Engine Size	1998cc
Cylinders	4
0-60 mph	2.9 secs
Top Speed	155mph
Power Output	245bhp
Transmission	Manual
Gears	6 speed
Length	134.25in (3410mm)
Width	70.78in (1798mm)
Height	47.04in (1195mm)
Weight	1102lb (500kg)
Wheelbase	92.3in (2345mm)

(Specifications refer to 2008 Ariel Atom 3)

but it can boast an exhilarating performance and head-turning looks; the racecar engineering and high-quality components deliver an unforgettable driving experience. While the handling of early models could be tricky at high speeds, Ariel have addressed the steering and balance to result in a responsive and thrilling sports car for the 21st century.

With Ariel only producing in the region of 100 cars each year, the Atom remains an exclusive model among sports car enthusiasts.

Aston Martin DB7

The Aston Martin DB7 is a two-door grand tourer that was engineered by TWR under instruction of Ford Motor Company (who owned Aston Martin until 2007). Available with a coupe or convertible bodystyle, the DB7 was offered as an entry-level vehicle to the Aston Martin brand and more than 7,000 examples of the car were sold before it was replaced by the DB9. With Ford's financial backing and components from Jaguar, development of the DB7 commenced. Using the platform of a Jaguar XJS, styling was handed over to chief designer and general manager Ian Callum who

completed the prototype in time for its unveiling at the 1993 Geneva Motor Show.

Both the coupe and convertible (*volante*) variants produced between 1997-1998 were powered by a 3.2-liter supercharged straight-six engine that could generate 335bhp and 361lb/ft of torque. In 1999 the DB7 V12 Vantage debuted at the Geneva Motor Show, boasting a 5.9-liter V12 engine derived from a Ford Duratec V6 that increased the power output to 420bhp and torque to 400lb/ft. Clients could also choose between a five-speed automatic gearbox and a TREMEC T-56 six-speed

Produced	1994-2004
Engine Size	3239cc
Cylinders	6
0-60 mph	6.2 secs
Top Speed	165mph
Power Output	335bhp
Transmission	Manual
Gears	5 speed
Length	182.9in (4646mm)
Width	72in (1829mm)
Height	48.7in (1237mm)
Weight	3889lb (1764kg)
Wheelbase	102in (2211mm)

(Specifications refer to 1997 Aston Martin DB7)

manual transmission. Performance-wise it was capable of achieving a 0-60 sprint in 4.9 seconds and could power on to 186mph (with manual transmission). The chassis was redesigned to cope with the increase of power. Cosmetically the DB7 still exuded the beauty of its earlier relative although the revised flanks, new rear bumper, and wider front grille gave a more masculine appearance. While some supercars appear flashy, the DB7 is one that oozes class and defines its driver as one with exquisite taste.

The V12 Vantage was well received and, as a result, Aston Martin saw reduced sales of the former supercharged engine variant, with clients favoring the new model. At the 2002 British International Motor Show, Aston Martin introduced their final and most powerful version of the DB7; the V12 GT (or V12 GTA when fitted with automatic transmission) offered an enhanced version of the Vantage that could produce 435bhp. Twin vents in the hood for dissipating heat, a rear spoiler and wheel arch liners to improve the aerodynamics, and a wire mesh front grille changed the aesthetics of the car. Aston Martin only produced 190 GTs and 112 GTAs worldwide, making it a rare and sought-after variant.

Aston Martin Vanquish

The Aston Martin Vanquish debuted at the 2001 Geneva Motor Show as a replacement for the Virage range and was available as either a two-seater or 2+2 setup. Similar to the DB7, the Vanquish was styled by Ian Callum and the two cars share many resemblances in their appearance. Since its conception the Vanquish model has been introduced in two generations – the first generation marked the arrival of the V12 Vanquish between 2001 and 2005, and the Vanquish S between 2004 and 2007. The powertrain in both these variants is a 6.0-liter 48-valve 60° mounted engine coupled with a six-speed electrohydraulic manual transmission but, while the V12 Vanquish generates 450bhp, the Vanquish S delivers an improved power output of 520bhp. Visually the Vanquish S had received some styling revisions including a slightly different nose shape and new wheels. The aerodynamics had also been improved through the addition of a small front splitter and an integrated trunk spoiler that housed a third high-level brake light. An optional sports dynamic pack offered sportier suspension, steering, and brakes.

The second generation of Vanquish models began in 2012 with the unveiling of the Project AM310 concept, which Aston Martin later announced would

Produced	2001-2007 and 2012 to present
Engine Size	5935cc
Cylinders	12
0-60 mph	4.1 secs
Top Speed	183mph
Power Output	565bhp
Transmission	Touchtronic 2 automatic
Gears	6 speed
Length	185.8in (4720mm)
Width	75in (1905mm)
Height	50.4in (1280mm)
Weight	3833lb (1739kg)
Wheelbase	83in (2211mm)

(Specifications refer to 2012 Aston Martin Vanquish)

be put into production under the resurrected Vanquish name as the ultimate grand tourer.

Inspiration from the Aston Martin DBS and the One-77 supercar led to the design that features sculpted curves and a carbon fiber body and, by using the new Generation 4 VH chassis that also utilizes carbon fiber, the all-new Vanquish is around 25 per cent lighter than the DBS while also demonstrating increased strength and rigidity.

It features Aston Martin's most powerful production engine to date – the new AM11 Gen4 V12. Generating 565bhp and 457lb/ft it offers the greatest performance seen in the Aston Martin fleet with acceleration from 0-60 in 4.1 seconds and a top speed of 183mph. The Vanquish enables the driver to select from three distinct modes (normal, sport, track) to tailor the driving experience and broaden the car's character. The interior offers exquisite luxury with integrated technology. Sumptuous supple leather seats are available in a range of colors and the advanced infotainment system allows complete control over the cabin environment. The new Aston Martin Vanquish has it all: performance, luxury, and technology.

Bugatti Veyron

Produced	2005 to present
Engine Size	7993cc
Cylinders	16
0-60 mph	2.46 secs
Top Speed	269mph
Power Output	1184bhp
Transmission	Dual clutch direct shift
Gears	7 speed
Length	175.7in (4462mm)
Width	78.7in (1998mm)
Height	45.6in (1159mm)
Weight	4162lb (1888kg)
Wheelbase	106.7in (2710mm)

(Specifications refer to 2010 Bugatti
Veyron Super Sport [SS])

The Bugatti Veyron is renowned
for its stylish looks and epic
performance. Plans for the Veyron
were unveiled at the 1999 Tokyo
Motor Show, but it was not until
2003 that a roadworthy prototype
had been created. However
technical issues with the prototype
had to be addressed so it was not
until 2005 that the car finally made
its way into production. The car
was named in honor of a Bugatti
development engineer, racing
driver, and company test driver
Pierre Veyron who won the 1939
24 Hours of Le Mans while driving
a Bugatti.

The original Veyron released in
2005 could boast a power output
of 1001bhp. The 16-cylinder
8.0-liter engine was essentially
formed by joining two V8 engines
at the crank. An impressive 0-60

performance of 2.5 seconds and a top speed of 253mph thrust the Veyron into record books as the fastest production road car. In order to tap into the immense power a special key is used; the car is lowered to a mere 3.5 inches from the ground while a hydraulic spoiler extends out. Despite its heavy weight, the Veyron offers surprisingly sharp handling. The distinctive shape of the Veyron remains unchanged except for two NACA ducts (developed by the National Advisory Committee for Aeronautics, hence the initials) placed in the roof rather than scoops above the engine, reshaped front air intakes that extend around the side of the wheel arch, and the centrally arranged exhaust system.

In 2010 Bugatti revealed the new Super Sport variant of the Veyron. Limited to just 30

examples, the Super Sport features a revised aerodynamic package. It is blisteringly fast; powered by an 8.0-liter quad turbocharged W16 cylinder engine, the Veyron SS unleashes a magnificent 1184bhp and 990lb/ft of torque enabling a 0-60 dash in just 2.46 seconds and can accelerate on to a top speed of 269mph. It is so fast that Bugatti have electronically limited the car from exceeding 258mph to protect the tires from disintegrating. For those that truly want a seriously limited edition, there is the Bugatti Veyron 16.4 Super Sport World Record Edition, which features a black exposed carbon fiber and orange body color – only five examples of the car have been made worldwide.

The Bugatti Veyron Super Sport has an eye-watering price tag of $2.7 million, ensuring that it remains a car only for the supreme elite.

Chevrolet Corvette C6 ZR1

Nicknamed "The Blue Devil" during production, the Chevrolet Corvette C6 ZR1 was created as a direct response to the Dodge Viper. It is the fastest and most powerful Corvette to date, and can demonstrate exceptional performance on the road or on the track. In 2010 it was the overall winner of the Car and Driver Lightning Lap competition. The two-door two-seater coupe is powered by a 6.2-liter LS9, a heavily modified version of the LS3 Corvette engine, and generates 638bhp and 604lb/ft of torque. The LS9 is equipped with a four-lobe Eaton TVS supercharger, with each cylinder bank having its own intercooler. Performance-

Produced	2009 to present
Engine Size	6162cc
Cylinders	8
0-60 mph	3.1 secs
Top Speed	205mph
Power Output	638bhp
Transmission	Manual
Gears	6 speed
Length	176.2in (4480mm)
Width	75.9in (1930mm)
Height	48.7in (1240mm)
Weight	3405lb (1544kg)
Wheelbase	105.7in (2680mm)

(Specifications refer to 2009 Chevrolet Corvette C6 ZR1)

wise the ZR1 can do 0-60 in an impressive 3.1 seconds and has a maximum speed of 205mph. It also boasts exceptional stopping ability, courtesy of the Brembo carbon ceramic brake rotors; weighing as much as 50 per cent less than cast-iron units, they are capable of operating at 1832° Fahrenheit (1000° Celsius) without warping.

Magnetic Selective Ride Control (MSRC) offers two modes of control – tour and sport –allowing the driver to select the preferred mode according to conditions and driving style. The MSRC shock absorbers are automatically adjusted every millisecond in response to corners, braking, and road conditions to offer optimal handling. The electromagnetic coil that resides inside each damper piston translates electrical current to stiffen suspension capabilities when necessary.

The chassis is aluminum, while much of the body, including the roof, fenders, and hood, is made out of carbon fiber panels to reduce weight. A clear coating is applied to protect the carbon fiber panels from sun damage. Classic Corvette design elements have provided the foundation for the ZR1's exterior. Its chiseled style and aggressive demeanor reflect its racing roots while the polycarbonate window above the supercharger in the carbon fiber hood gives a striking appearance. ZR1 owners are able

to put their own personalized stamp on their car by selecting their preferred choice of brake caliper color: standard blue, red, yellow, dark gray, or silver. In addition to this, headlamps are available in gray, silver, or black.

Retailing between $111,525 and $129,945 the Chevrolet Corvette C6 ZR1 is surprisingly good value for money when compared to a Porsche Carrera GT that offers similar performance for more than twice the price.

Dodge Viper

In 1996 the second generation of Dodge Vipers were unveiled: the Phase II SR Viper RT/10 and GTS. In addition to a newly released roadster, a coupe variant was also produced that was nicknamed "double bubble" in reference to the raised sections of roof that were designed to accommodate helmet usage. Since their initial conception, Vipers have been involved in both drag racing and road racing.

The GTS still shared many visual similarities to its predecessor, but overall the car had experienced some major modifications. A completely new chassis was designed that was 25 per cent stiffer in torsional rigidity but lighter by 60lb (27kg). The suspension was revised and this, coupled with the stiffer chassis and more aerodynamic body, increased the car's lateral grip.

The engine had been reworked to offer enhanced power – the 8.0-liter V10 being capable of producing 450bhp and increasing the top speed by 5mph to 185mph in comparison to a first-generation Viper.

The brakes initially lacked ABS and were the weakest factor in the second-generation Viper. In a supercar comparison the Viper GTS was placed last for brake efficiency, demonstrating much longer stopping distances than its rivals. However, it was placed in the top position for many other performance exercises, beating the likes of the Ferrari 355 and the Porsche 911 Turbo. In 1999, the Viper was revised and featured some minor changes; new 18-inch diameter wheels and tires were

added, and an improved exhaust system replaced the side exhaust, which was subsequently dropped from the design. The 1999 edition also boasted a refined interior including Cognac Connolly leather seats. ABS was finally introduced to the vehicle in 2001 and, a year later during the Viper GTS' final year in production, the 360 commemorative "final edition"

Produced	1996-2002
Engine Size	7998cc
Cylinders	10
0-60 mph	4 secs
Top Speed	185mph
Power Output	450bhp
Transmission	Manual
Gears	6 speed
Length	175.1in (4450mm)
Width	75.7in (1920mm)
Height	44in (1120mm)
Weight	3375lb (1531kg)
Wheelbase	96.2in (2440mm)

(Specifications refer to 1996-1997 Viper GTS)

models were released. As homage to the famous race-winning Oreca cars (who worked closely with Dodge) the final models were painted red with white stripes.

The Viper was exported to Europe under the Chrysler badge and during its years in production more than 10,000 examples of the car were sold worldwide. 2002 marked the end of the second generation to make way for the RT/10s replacement, the SRT-10 in 2003, while replacement for the GTS did not arrive until 2006 with the SRT-10 Coupe.

Ferrari Enzo (F60)

Ferrari have always utilized race-derived technology for application in the development of their production cars, but the F60 (dubbed the Ferrari Enzo) offers the perfect fusion of technology for both road and track applications. The limited edition run of F60s simultaneously marked the start of a new generation of V12 engines while celebrating the company's Formula One prowess. The completely new rear-mounted 65° V12 delivers intense power and massive torque at low revs; with a displacement of 5998cc the engine punches out a maximum power output of 660bhp at 7800rpm. Designed by Ken Okuyama from Pininfarina, the Enzo was subject to extensive wind tunnel and track testing, which influenced the streamlined shape, while a carbon fiber body, ceramic composite disc brakes, and a F1-style

electrohydraulic shift transmission demonstrates the Formula One technology that has been applied. The six-speed electrohydraulic system automatically disengages the clutch, activates a gear change, and orders a burst of torque from the engine in just 150ms. The F60 also features traction control and active aerodynamics to generate exceptional downforce. In terms of performance the Enzo can accelerate from 0-60 in a mere 3.4 seconds and can reach an impressive 217mph.

The 60th-anniversary model was named Enzo in honor of the founder, Enzo Ferrari, who believed that the design of production cars should be influenced by racers. When production of the Enzo was first announced, Ferrari had initially stated that they would build 349 examples of the car. Only those deemed worthy of Ferrari's new

creation were invited to purchase one, and the company prioritized clients that had previously bought one of the anniversary models, such as the F40 or F50. The Enzo proved exceptionally popular and all 349 cars were sold before production began so Ferrari announced that a

Produced	2002-2004
Engine Size	5998cc
Cylinders	12
0-60 mph	3.4 secs
Top Speed	217mph
Power Output	660bhp
Transmission	Semi-automatic
Gears	6 speed
Length	185.1in (4702mm)
Width	80.1in (2035mm)
Height	45.2in (1147mm)
Weight	3020lb (1370kg)
Wheelbase	104.3in (2650mm)

(Specifications refer to 2002 Ferrari Enzo)

further 50 Enzos would be built. Buyers were invited to the factory so that their new car could receive a tailor-made cockpit that reflected their individual needs, including positioning of the accelerator and brake pedals. In 2004 Ferrari produced a 400th car, specially built to be auctioned for charity.

Auctioned by Sotheby's the top-of-the-range Enzo fetched $1.1 million – double the original retail price.

The Enzo has also been used as the starting point for other vehicles, such as the Ferrari FXX and P4/5 as well as the Maserati MC12 (Ferrari owned a 50 per cent share in the company between 1997 and 2005).

Ferrari Testarossa

Produced	1984-1996
Engine Size	4943cc
Cylinders	12
0-60 mph	5.2 secs
Top Speed	180mph
Power Output	390bhp
Transmission	Manual
Gears	5 speed
Length	176.6in (4485mm)
Width	77.8in (1976mm)
Height	44.5in (1130mm)
Weight	3320lb (1506kg)
Wheelbase	100.4in (2550mm)

(Specifications refer to the Testarossa base model)

Ferrari unveiled their Pininfarina-designed Testarossa at the 1984 Paris Motor Show. Powered by a mid-mounted 4.9-liter Ferrari Colombo flat-12 engine that reached a top speed of 180mph and a 0-60 of 5.2 seconds, the Testarossa quickly became another of Ferrari's iconic production cars.

The Testarossa featured many radical design changes to its predecessor, the Ferrari Berlinetta Boxer, some of which had been the trademark styling of many Ferrari models for decades. Unlike the sharp and boxy front-end look seen on earlier models, a more rounded and softer approach had been explored. The striking and somewhat innovative design of the side air intakes gave the vehicle its iconic look; it was the twin side-mounted radiators that required the additional cooling provided by the tapering ventilation.

As a result of the Testarossa's mid-engine placement, which created a perfect gravitational balance between the front and rear axles, the car boasted a standing

weight distribution of 40 per cent to the front and 60 per cent to the rear; this feature assisted with better cornering and the general stability of the car on the road. A further radical design change was that of the singular exterior mirror mounted on the driver's side of the vehicle. While this was displeasing to some, it was not until 1987, during the Geneva Motor Show, that it was announced that the placement of the mirror had been changed to a more suitable position and matched by a passenger side accompaniment. In 1991 the standard Testarossa model was replaced by the 512 TR, which featured a better weight distribution (41 per cent to the front and 59 per cent to the rear), alongside larger intake valves, a

better engine management system, and a broader power curve to assist with better acceleration. Later in 1995 the industry also saw the introduction of the F512 M – a more evenly weight distributed version of the 512 TR. By the time that the cars ware removed from the production line, Ferrari had manufactured close to 10,000 from the Testarossa, 512 TR, and F512 M lines, making this series one of the most popular and widely sold Ferraris at the time.

Ford GT

Produced	2004-2006
Engine Size	5409cc
Cylinders	8
0-60 mph	3.6 secs
Top Speed	205mph
Power Output	550bhp
Transmission	Manual
Gears	6 speed
Length	182.8in (4640mm)
Width	76.9in (1950mm)
Height	44.3in (1130mm)
Weight	3351lb (1520kg)
Wheelbase	106.7in (2710mm)

(Specifications refer to 2004 Ford GT)

Displayed as a concept car at the 2002 North American Auto Show, the Ford GT conjured up nostalgic images of the company's GT racecars from the 1960s. It had been designed as part of a showcase to revive heritage names and marked Ford's 100th anniversary. Designed in secret under the name "Petunia," the concept car brought the GT40 back to life as a street-legal car and is known internally as "the American supercar reborn."

While the Ford GT bears an external resemblance to the original Ford GT40 cars, there are no structural similarities. The GT uses many unique techniques including a super-plastic-formed frame and aluminum body panels. It features four-piston aluminum Brembo monobloc brake calipers that work with cross-drilled and vented rotors. A double-wishbone suspension with unequal-length aluminum control arms, and coil-over monotube shock absorbers are used front and rear.

The mid-mounted 5.4-liter modular V8 engine is coupled with an Eaton supercharger positioned low in the car's frame due to the use of a dry sump oiling system. This choice of positioning also helped to keep the car's center of gravity low in order to achieve better handling and balance. The GT boasted the all-new, six-speed Ricardo transmission which, coupled with the supercharged engine, meant the GT was capable of generating a power output of 550bhp, and torque of 500lb/ft, and demonstrated a 0-60 sprint in 3.6 seconds and a top speed of 205mph.

The aerodynamic development of the car included wind tunnel testing to ensure that each air intake and heat extractor on the car was fully functional. Side intakes were enlarged to ensure that cooling air was driven into the engine,

while additional vents were added to either side of the rear glass to diffuse excess heat from the engine compartment. Each line and curve of the body contributes to the modern-day interpretation of the original racer as opposed to a reproduction of its styling.

The interior of the car gives a nod to the vintage endurance racers by featuring analog gauges and stylized toggle switches on the instrument panel, while the leather seats are dotted with aluminum grommets to provide ventilation.

Gumpert Apollo

The story of the Gumpert Apollo begins in 2000 when former Audi engineer Roland Gumpert proposed to design a street-legal car that was racetrack ready. Following the initial designs produced by Marco Vanetta, a 1:4 scale model of the Apollo was created in 2002. The objective was clear, to design and build a supercar that utilizes traditional hand-built craftsmanship and blend it with cutting-edge technology. The Gumpert Sportwagenmanufaktur company was founded in 2004 and development of the Apollo continued with the Technical University of Munich and Ingolstadt University of Applied Sciences. In addition to their constructional input, extensive wind tunnel testing and computer simulations provided the results required to produce the first prototypes. In 2005 production officially commenced, and the Apollo made its racing debut in the Divinol Cup at the Hockenheimring racetrack.

Each Apollo is constructed to the owner's individual specifications. The exterior boasts sumptuous curves and angular edges with the sole purpose of being aerodynamically uncompromised. Gumpert have claimed that the design of the Apollo generates enough downforce for the car to be driven upside down in a tunnel when driving above 190mph, however this is yet to be tested!

The Apollo is constructed on a tubular spaceframe in chrome molybdenum steel, with fiberglass or optional carbon fiber body panels. The 4.0-liter twin-turbo intercooled engine is a modified version of the Audio V8. The 90° V8 engine is mid-mounted and comes in three types: base, sport, and race. With a power output of between 650 and 800bhp, the Apollo boasts an exceptional 0-60 performance of just 3.1 seconds – and that is just the base model. The Apollo Sport shaves milliseconds off the time, producing a 0-60 dash in a mere 2.9 seconds. The Apollo Sport also comes equipped with an extended aerodynamic package to increase downforce further by adding a racing wing. In 2008 Gumpert announced that a hybrid version of the Apollo would be competing at the 24 Hours Nürburgring and within three months the car was completed. Powered by a 3.3-liter V8 twin-turbo engine, and coupled with an electric motor that can generate 134bhp, the overall power output of the hybrid Apollo is 512bhp.

The Apollo may not be defined as a classically beautiful car and what it lacks in heritage it makes up for with bold and aggressive looks, epic power, and thrilling performance.

Produced	2005 to present
Engine Size	4163cc
Cylinders	8
0-60 mph	2.9 secs
Top Speed	223.9mph
Power Output	690bhp
Transmission	Sequential manual
Gears	6 speed
Length	175.6in (4460mm)
Width	78.7in (1998mm)
Height	43.9in (1114mm)
Weight	2400-2600lb (1100-1200kg)
Wheelbase	106.3in (2700mm)

(Specifications refer to 2005 Gumpert Apollo Sport)

Hennessey Venom GT

Produced	2012 to present
Engine Size	6205cc
Cylinders	8
0-60 mph	2.7 secs
Top Speed	270mph
Power Output	1244bhp
Transmission	Manual
Gears	6 speed
Length	183.3in (4655mm)
Width	77.2in (1960mm)
Height	42.5in (1079mm)
Weight	2743lb (1244kg)
Wheelbase	110.2in (2800mm)

(Specifications refer to 2014 Hennessey Venom GT)

The Hennessey Venom GT first made its appearance in spring 2010. The concept for the Venom GT arose after John Hennessey joked about putting the engine from a Venom 1000 twin-turbo Viper into the back of an Exige. His initial aim was to improve the performance of the Viper but he was unable to add more power via the front-engine rear-wheel drive platform, and the weight could not be reduced by more than 200lb, so he began looking at other lightweight models that could house the twin-turbo V8 engine. His joke soon evaporated as he looked at the sketches and realized that there was potential in an Exige platform. The Venom GT utilizes its chassis (albeit heavily modified) among other components including the roof, doors, windscreen, side glass, and headlamps. By distributing the weight of the engine and transmission over the rear tires, better traction is offered. The engine output is adjustable using a programmable traction control system that features three settings: 800, 1000, 1244bhp.

The mid-engined V8 coupled with the Ricardo six-speed manual transmission results in a maximum speed of 270mph and, in February 2014, the Venom GT smashed the Bugatti Veyron's record as the fastest car in the world. However, the *Guinness Book of Records* have not accepted the performance – to be eligible an average is taken from two runs and the Venom GT only

completed a single run. It does also not qualify as a series production car as only 11 examples have been manufactured, to date.

The team responsible for the design and styling can boast a rich history in motorsport including Formula One and Le Mans so it's no surprise that their race-derived technology has been applied to the Venom GT. It boasts carbon fiber bodywork to reduce weight as well as an adjustable suspension system to allow different height adjustments according to driving conditions and speed. The Venom GT also features active aerodynamics and an adjustable rear wing. Optional upgrades include Michelin Pilot Sport Cup ZP tires, bare carbon fiber finish, and a stereo system designed by Steven Tyler, the lead singer of Aerosmith.

Prices start at $1.2 million and production for the GT is limited, with Hennessey producing only 29 examples of the car each year.

Jaguar XJ220

Produced	1992-1994
Engine Size	3498cc
Cylinders	6
0-60 mph	3.6 secs
Top Speed	217mph
Power Output	542bhp
Transmission	Manual
Gears	5 speed
Length	194.1in (4930mm)
Width	87.4in (2220mm)
Height	45.3in (1150mm)
Weight	3241lb (1470kg)
Wheelbase	103.9in (2640mm)

(Specifications refer to 1992
Jaguar XJ220)

The concept version of the Jaguar XJ220 debuted at the British International Motor Show in 1988 where it was positively received. It had been developed by a group of 12 volunteers that became known as "The Saturday Club." Considering the FIA Group B regulations the design followed a mid-engine configuration, four-wheel drive layout, and was to be powered by a V12 engine. It had a targeted top speed of 220mph, hence the XJ220. Featuring scissor doors (as seen on Lamborghinis), covered headlamps, and a wide array of interior luxuries including Connolly leather seats, electric windows, air conditioning, and an Alpine Electronics CD player, the XJ220 was a high-specification supercar that was both sumptuous and stylish.

Following its successful public appearance and more than 1,500 deposits being collected, production of the XJ220 commenced. However, the early 1990s recession and significant changes to the car's specifications had a negative effect on sales, resulting in Jaguar only producing 275 examples.

The production version of the XJ220 was finally shown to the public at the Tokyo Motor Show in 1991. The two-seater coupe was Jaguar's first production supercar – although they had previously produced racing vehicles and striking concept cars, this was the first to push the threshold of performance while also being production ready.

Powered by a 3.5-liter twin-turbo variant of the Austin Rover/TWR V64V V6 engine developed by TWR, the XJ220 was capable of generating 542bhp. Coupled with the five-speed transmission, it could boast a 0-60 performance of 3.6 seconds and had a top speed of 217mph. Before going into production it was decided that the XJ220 would not utilize four-wheel drive as initially planned. Jim Randle and Keith Helfet were responsible for styling and used inspiration from Le Mans racing cars. The scissor doors were dropped in favor of regular doors, and a number of minor design changes were tested in the wind tunnel to ensure maximum efficiency with regard to aerodynamics. The XJ220 was one of the first production cars to generate downforce through intentional underbody flow and the Venturi effect (the reduction in fluid pressure that results when a fluid flows through a constricted section of pipe).

The Jaguar XJ220 held the record as the world's fastest production car until 1993 when the McLaren F1 beat it.

Koenigsegg CCR

Produced	2004-2006
Engine Size	4700cc
Cylinders	8
0-60 mph	3.7 secs
Top Speed	241mph
Power Output	806bhp
Transmission	Manual
Gears	6 speed
Length	165in (4190mm)
Width	78.3in (1990mm)
Height	42.1in (1070mm)
Weight	2712lb (1230kg)
Wheelbase	104.7in (2660mm)

(Specifications refer to 2004
Koenigsegg CCR)

The Koenigsegg CCR made its
public debut at the 2004 Geneva
Auto Show as a successor to the
CC8S. Although it shared several
similarities with the CC8S, with the

dihedral synchro-helix actuation
doors being the most obvious, the
body received some significant
upgrades, including a large front
splitter for increased downforce
and the underside being completely
flat in order to achieve better
aerodynamics. In addition to these
the body of the CCR also featured
new headlamps and redesigned
side air intakes, improving the
amount of air that gets pulled in to
maximize efficiency of the oil cooler
and intercooler.

Powered by a 4.7-liter 90° mid-
longitudinally mounted V8 engine
that generates a staggering 806bhp,
the CCR boasts a 0-60 dash in
3.7 seconds. Larger brakes and an
upgraded suspension contribute
to the racing car qualities that it

possesses. The brakes have been
specially developed for the model
by AP-Racing. Unlike standard
discs, which are mounted in a
fixed position, they are configured
in a "floating mount" that allows
fractional movement in all directions.
This, coupled with the Koenigsegg
brake ventilation system, means the
brakes are remarkably stable.

The CCR is equipped with
custom-built shock absorbers,
specifically developed for the
model by Italian firm VPS. Usually
produced for racing vehicles, the
shocks are lightweight and allow
for extensive fine-tuning to suit
driving preferences, whether they
are on road or track. The CCR is
adorned with a symbol of a ghost
in honor of the Swedish Fighter Jet

Squadron No.1 that had occupied the Koenigsegg facility.

The CCR previously held the title as the world's fastest production car, after successfully breaking the record that had been held by the McLaren F1. Driven by Loris Bicocchi at the Nardo Track in Italy, the CCR achieved a top speed of 241mph. However, the victory was short lived as two months later the Bugatti Veyron knocked it from top position with a top speed of over 249mph.

Koenigsegg only produced 14 examples of the CCR, making it one of the rarest Koenigsegg models to date.

Lamborghini Countach

Produced	1974-1990
Engine Size	3929cc
Cylinders	12
0-60 mph	6.8 secs
Top Speed	180mph
Power Output	375bhp
Transmission	Manual
Gears	5 speed
Length	163in (4140mm)
Width	74.4in (1890mm)
Height	42.1in (1070mm)
Weight	3020lb (1370kg)
Wheelbase	95.5in (2450mm)

(Specifications refer to 1974 Lamborghini Countach LP400)

The Lamborghini Countach was an evolutionary car throughout almost two decades in production. Styled by Bertone designer Marcello Gandini, the Lamborghini Countach may have lacked a number of practical and ergonomic aspects of automotive design, but its striking demeanor and wedge-shaped angular body was pioneering, and popularized the look that a number of high-performance cars mimicked. The sunflower yellow prototype made its debut at the 1971 Geneva Motor Show and featured all of Gandini's original design concepts, however the production model adopted a number of minor changes in order to improve its performance, handling, and tractability.

The Countach features a tubular spaceframe, covered in aircraft-grade aluminum and fiberglass underbody resulting in a strong but lightweight vehicle. The angular shape is wide and low with the majority of the body made out of trapezoid panels and Lamborghini's now famous trademark scissor doors, which were first used on the Countach.

NACA ducts were featured on the door and rear fenders of each side of the car, and a large engine vent became necessary for adequate cooling. In contrast to the transversely mounted engine of the Miura, the Countach features a traditional Lamborghini V12 engine mounted longitudinally.

European models were equipped with six Weber carburetors whereas US variants used Bosch K-Jetronic fuel injection.

In 1978 Lamborghini released the new LP 400S model, which featured a number of exterior changes to improve the car's handling and stability at high speeds. Pirelli P7 units replaced the original tires, and fiberglass wheel arches were added. An optional V-shaped spoiler was mounted at the rear and, although this improved stability, it also reduced the top speed by 10mph. Four years later a revised model called the LP 500S was released – although aesthetically it remained unchanged, it featured a more powerful 4.8-liter engine.

Lamborghini continued to enhance the powertrain of the Countach throughout its production years. In 1988 they released the 25th anniversary Countach to celebrate Lamborghini's quarter of a century milestone. The air intakes on the rear of the car had become larger, while a new air dam and side skirting was fitted. The final edition proved to be immensely popular and was the fastest variant of the Countach, performing a 0-60 sprint in a commendable 4.7 seconds and boasting a top speed of 183mph.

Lamborghini Diablo

Codenamed "Project 132," the development of the Diablo was first initiated back in 1985 as a replacement for Lamborghini's Countach model. Like many other Lamborghini models, the Diablo took its name from a breed of fighting bull: Diablo is a direct translation of the word "devil" in Spanish. The first edition of the legendary futuristic production vehicle was unveiled in 1990 at the Hotel de Paris (Monte-Carlo), which turned the heads of car fanatics and critics alike, drawing attention to its astounding body shape and aerodynamic design. Aside from its dashing aesthetic

value, the Diablo was also the first Lamborghini ever built to have exceeded 200mph as its top speed. The rear-wheel-driven sports car boasted an impressive 5.7-liter V12 that punched out an incredible 492bhp, with a torque rating of 428lb/ft. The longitudinally mid-mounted engine was strategically placed to assist with the vehicle's balance ratio (of 41 per cent to the front and 59 per cent to the rear) and produced a top recorded speed of 204mph and a 0-60 in just 4.09 seconds.

The first design of the Diablo was commissioned to Marcello Gandini who had also designed

the Countach and the Miura. However, after Chrysler had purchased the company in 1987, Gandini's designs were sent to a third party for refinement, much to the designer's disappointment. Gandini however did go on to realize his initial concept and design in the Cizeta-Moroder V16T in 1991. As standard, the Diablo was constructed from a high-resistance steel alloy and carbon fiber frame, with an aluminum alloy and hand layup of composite materials for the bodywork. Originally priced at $239,000, the Diablo was obviously built for the upper end of the market of supercar and

Produced	1990-2001
Engine Size	5707cc
Cylinders	12
0-60 mph	4.09 secs
Top Speed	204mph
Power Output	492bhp
Transmission	Manual
Gears	5 speed
Length	175.3in (4460mm)
Width	80.2in (2040mm)
Height	43.4in (1105mm)
Weight	3475lb (1576kg)
Wheelbase	104.3in (2650mm)

(Specifications refer to 1990 Lamborghini Diablo)

sports car enthusiasts. After several developments of the first edition of the Diablo, Lamborghini produced various models in the vehicle's lengthy production run, including the Diablo, Diablo VT, Diablo SE30 and SE30 Jota, Diablo SV, Diablo VT Roadster, Diablo SV, Diablo SV SE35, Diablo VT and VT Roadster, Diablo GT, Diablo VT 6.0 and VT 6.0 SE, proving that "project 132" was indeed a worthy investment for the car maker, where over 2,800 units had been produced. The Diablo was finally retired in 2001, where the Murciélago would then take its place as the company's newest offering.

Lamborghini Miura

The Lamborghini Miura (also known as the P400) was the brainchild of its designer Marcello Gandini who unveiled the car at the Geneva Motor Show in 1966, taking onlookers and the automotive market by storm. The name Miura is again taken from the company's ritual of naming models after a famous fighting bull. During its production period the Miura became Lamborghini's flagship production vehicle, despite it being developed against the company founder's wishes: while an engineering team built the car behind closed doors, Ferruccio Lamborghini had wanted to focus on the production of powerful grand touring vehicles.

At the time of release the Miura was considered by many to be the

Produced	1966-1972
Engine Size	3929cc
Cylinders	12
0-60 mph	6.3 secs
Top Speed	163mph
Power Output	350bhp
Transmission	Manual
Gears	5 speed
Length	172.8in (4390mm)
Width	70.1 n (1780mm)
Height	43.3in (1100mm)
Weight	2601lb (1180kg)
Wheelbase	98.6in (2504mm)

(Specifications refer to 1968 Lamborghini Miura P400)

"first" supercar, with its hitherto unseen engineering of the 1960s; both visually and technologically the P400 made other leading sports car manufacturers look outdated.

The powerful 3.9-liter V12 had the capacity to punch out an impressive 350bhp, a top speed of 163mph, and 0-60 in 6.3 seconds. The lightweight chassis and sleek aerodynamic body contouring meant that the Miura was quick on the road and lighter than many of its direct automotive competitors.

The car was essentially released as a marketing ploy to gain more interest for the company and was later made famous by its appearance in the original version of the 1969 box office hit *The Italian Job*, where the P400 featured in the opening sequence. The Miura boasted a transversely mounted mid-engine that had not previously featured in any Lamborghini predecessor and also the V12 was formed in a single casting alongside the transmission

(as seen in earlier models of the Mini). The P400 was constructed using a steel frame and door paneling, with aluminum front and rear body panels. Early units off the production line were fitted with a wooden steering wheel and gear knob, helping to prove their authenticity and production year. A surprising 275 units of the first production P400 model were produced between 1966 and 1969, an impressive sales record considering its then pricey retail value. Lamborghini later introduced the Countach in 1974, which saw production of the Miura come to an end. Overall, the manufacturer had produced 764 units of the P400, including its slightly modified variants in the Miura series, including the P400, P400S, P400SV, P400 Jota, and the P400 SV/J.

Maserati Bora

The Maserati Bora was unveiled at the Geneva Motor Show in 1971 and went into production shortly after. Once again Maserati turned to Giorgetto Giugiaro at Italdesign for the styling after he designed the successful predecessor – the Maserati Ghibli.

The concept of a two-seater sports car came shortly after Citroën took a controlling interest in Maserati. The Bora was the first mid-engine production car for the company, and was designed to compete against the Lamborghini

Produced	1971-1978
Engine Size	4930cc
Cylinders	8
0-60 mph	6.6 secs
Top Speed	177mph
Power Output	330bhp
Transmission	Manual
Gears	5 speed
Length	171.5in (4355mm)
Width	69.6in (1768mm)
Height	44.6in (1134mm)
Weight	3569lb (1619kg)
Wheelbase	102.4in (2600mm)

(Specifications refer to 1971 Maserati Bora)

Miura, which five years earlier had popularized the use of the mid-engine layout.

With Citroën on board, the Bora took advantage of a number of the French manufacturer's components including retractable headlamps, leather covered bucket seats, and an adjustable pedal block. They also utilized the advanced high-pressure hydraulic system that operated the ventilated disc brakes. The combined body structure was a monocoque chassis and tubular steel subframe that housed the

engine and transmission.

Powered by a 4.9-liter V8 that is longitudinally mounted in front of the ZF five-speed transmission, the Bora was capable of generating 330bhp, although US models demonstrated a power output of 300bhp due to restrictions on emissions. It boasted a superb top speed of 177mph and could achieve a 0-60 performance in 6.6 seconds.

Unlike other supercars that offered very little practicality, the Bora addressed these issues to ensure that it offered adequate legroom, while a full-size trunk presented space for luggage at the front of the vehicle. The Bora also delivered superior comfort for the driver; with the touch of a button the pedal block could be moved backward or forward, and the steering wheel tilted, enabling easy access to the driver's seat.

In 1973 Maserati developed the racing version of the Bora to compete in Group Four classes, however they were unsuccessful in initially producing the 500 cars required for homologation. Production of the Bora stopped in 1978, after a total of 564 examples had been built. Tax restrictions introduced by the Italian government and the oil crisis had a negative impact on the market for high-performance vehicles, which inevitably had a knock-on effect for the Maserati Bora.

Maserati MC12

The MC12 signaled Maserati's return to racing after a 37-year absence. The two-seater sports car was designed using the chassis of the notorious Ferrari Enzo, although the MC12 ended up being much larger and featured a more pronounced nose and smoother curves than the Enzo. The increased size of the car resulted in greater downforce, aided by the large rear-mounted spoiler.

The production of this sports car intended to meet eligibility requirements from the FIA GT by producing at least 25 road-going examples – a total of 50 cars were built and sold with a retail price of $600,000 each. Although they were victorious at the Zhuhai International Circuit in 2004, they were exceeding size restrictions of the American Le Mans Series races and were subject to weight penalties.

The chassis is made from carbon fiber and Nomex, with an aluminum sub-chassis at the front and rear to support with bumps while also offering excellent safety

Produced	2004-2005
Engine Size	5998cc
Cylinders	12
0-60 mph	3.7 secs
Top Speed	205mph
Power Output	623bhp
Transmission	Maserati Cambiocorsa semi-automatic
Gears	6 speed
Length	202.5in (5143mm)
Width	82.5in (2096mm)
Height	47.4in (1205mm)
Weight	2943lb (1335kg)
Wheelbase	110.2in (2800mm)

(Specifications refer to 2004 Maserati MC12)

standards. The body of the two-door coupe is constructed entirely of carbon fiber and features a targa-top roof panel. Extensive wind tunnel testing combined with countless hours on the road and track helped to determine the best aerodynamic properties the car should feature; the underside is smooth while diffusers in the rear bumper aid downforce. The two-meter-wide spoiler affects the weight distribution above 125mph, adjusting the standing weight from 41 per cent front/59 per cent rear to 34 per cent front/66 per cent rear.

The MC12 is powered by a 6.0-liter Ferrari-derived V12 engine mounted at 65° positioned mid-

longitudinally. It is coupled with the rear-mounted six-speed semi-automatic transmission found in the Ferrari Enzo, although it is tuned to different gear ratios and renamed Maserati Cambiocorsa. Offering computerized gear selection, the Maserati Cambiocorsa electro-hydraulic transmission is selected via paddles mounted behind the

steering wheel. Two transmission modes are available: sport and race. The 0-60 dash is performed in 3.7 seconds and the MC12 can power on to a top speed of 205mph.

The MC12 boasts Brembo-developed brakes with a Bosch antilock braking system (ABS); the large ventilated cross-drilled discs deliver maximum braking efficiency.

McLaren F1

The McLaren F1 was an innovative creation that pushed the boundaries of sports car engineering. It boasted a number of groundbreaking technologies and utilized various high-quality materials including carbon fiber, gold, Kevlar, magnesium, and titanium, and was the first production car to use a carbon fiber monocoque chassis. It features a unique 1+2 seating arrangement that positions the driver in the center of the car to enhance the driving experience and ensures that they are in complete control and have the best possible view – like in a racing car. This unusual layout also meant that the McLaren F1 was the first supercar to offer room for two passengers.

Boasting performance pedigree from their highly successful Formula One engineering team and analysis of existing supercar performance characteristics, McLaren set out to produce a production car with uncompromising design. Its streamlined structure was stripped of any unnecessary weight; they reduced drag and increased downforce in order to create a breathtaking supercar that would deliver exceptional power to weight ratio while maintaining usability for everyday driving.

McLaren decided against the use of turbochargers and favored a naturally aspirated engine to power the F1. BMW's motorsport engineers developed the 6.1-liter V12 specifically for the F1. It generated the highest power output for its size, resulting in 627bhp, and since the carbon fiber body panels and monocoque chassis required substantial heat insulation the engine bay was lined with pure gold foil. Extensive craftsmanship went into the construction of each car; the throttle pedal was crafted from six pieces of titanium, the

Produced	1992-1998
Engine Size	6064cc
Cylinders	12
0-60 mph	3.2 secs
Top Speed	240mph
Power Output	627bhp
Transmission	Manual
Gears	6 speed
Length	168.8in (4288mm)
Width	71.7in (1820 mm)
Height	44.9in (1140mm)
Weight	2513lb (1140kg)
Wheelbase	107in (2718mm)

(Specifications refer to 1992 McLaren F1)

instrument panels were handmade and hand painted, and more than 3,000 hours were spent constructing each carbon fiber chassis. Wheels made from magnesium alloy reduced weight and provided excellent heat conduction.

Unlike many other supercars, the McLaren F1 doesn't utilize spoilers or wings in their aerodynamic approach, instead months of extensive wind tunnel testing contributed to their design while a Formula One flat underbody and diffuser system improves downforce. The F1 also boasts race-bred monitoring with the onboard diagnostic computer that sends data directly to McLaren.

The McLaren F1 held the record as the world's fastest production car for more than 10 years (the longest record), until the Bugatti

Veyron knocked it from the top spot. However the F1 still holds the record as the world's fastest *naturally aspirated* production car.

McLaren P1

Using Formula One technology and hybrid power, the McLaren P1 is the eagerly awaited successor to the McLaren F1 – a car that pushed the boundaries of innovation. The P1 follows the same rear-wheel drive, mid-engine design that was seen on the F1. It also shares the same carbon fiber monocoque and roof structure safety cage concept called the MonoCage, which features an integrated roof snorkel that is designed to draw in cold air to cool the engine.

The concept car debuted at the 2012 Paris Motor Show, drawing its technological and spiritual inspiration from McLaren's highly successful racing division. A year later the production version of the P1 was unveiled at the Geneva Motor Show. To retain total

Produced	2013 to present
Engine Size	3799cc
Cylinders	8
0-60 mph	2.6 secs
Top Speed	217mph (electronically limited)
Power Output	903bhp (combined with electric motor)
Transmission	SSG automatic
Gears	7 speed
Length	180.6in (4588mm)
Width	76.6in (1946 mm)
Height	46.8in (1188mm)
Weight	3197lb (1450kg)
Wheelbase	105.1in (2670 mm)

(Specifications refer to 2013 McLaren P1)

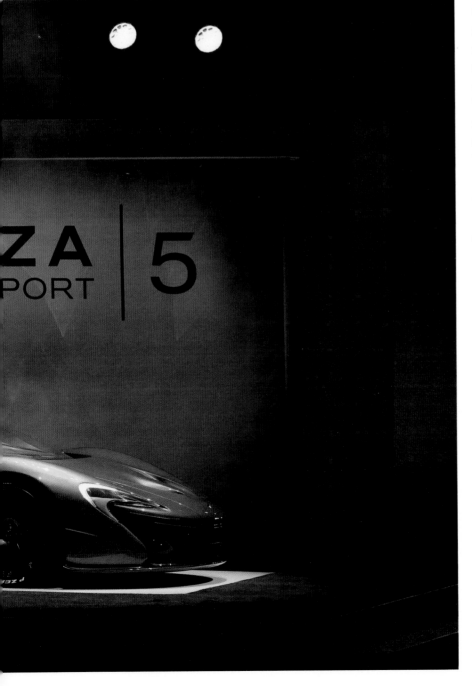

exclusivity McLaren announced that only 375 examples of the car would be built, with pricing starting at $1,350,000. By November 2013 all of the units had been sold.

Powered by a 3.8-liter twin-turbocharged V8 engine and coupled with an electric motor the P1 has an impressive power output of 903bhp and 722lb/ft of torque. The car can be powered by the petrol engine, the electric motor, or a combination of the two. While in E-mode (fully electric) the P1 is suited to city driving – it is near silent and is the most economical mode, however the battery is limited to a mere six miles of driving before it requires recharging. At this point the petrol engine springs into life. The P1 offers exhilarating performance, boasting a 0-60 sprint in an incredible 2.6 seconds and a top speed that has been electronically limited to 217mph.

Formula One technology is extensively used in the P1 with features such as the Instant Power Assist System (IPAS), which boosts acceleration from the electric motor, and a Drag Reduction System (DRS), which operates the rear wing on the car. The P1 also utilizes regenerative braking via the kinetic energy recovery system (KERS).

Its precise shape was born in the wind tunnel to develop the streamlined body and sculpted air intakes. It is aerodynamically advanced, using the active aero to maximize cooling while simultaneously boosting performance. The variable ride height allows the car to adapt to suit its environment and as speed increases the rear wing rises to create more downforce; in contrast the rear wing decreases slightly once speeds over 156mph are achieved as the colossal weight of the air passing over it would be too much for the suspension.

Mercedes-Benz SLR McLaren

Inspired by the Mercedes-Benz 300 SLR sports racing car that won the 1955 World Sportscar Championship, Mercedes collaborated with Formula One partner McLaren to design and build a grand tourer that would revive the glorious tradition of the SLR (Sport Light Racing). Introduced in the fall of 2003, the Mercedes-Benz SLR McLaren is a showcase of the extensive collective experience of the development and production of high-performance sports cars.

It boasts the perfect blend of innovation, technology, performance, and practicality. The powerplant is the Mercedes-AMG V8, with a displacement of 5439cc that generates a power output of 626bhp and torque of 575lb/ft at 1750rpm. This translates to an exceptional performance – a 0-60 sprint in just 3.6 seconds and a magnificent top speed of 207.5mph. The V8 engine is front-mid-mounted to offer the best possible weight distribution and stability on braking. The five-speed manual transmission has been designed for high performance, and has been optimized for high torque. It also features a Speedshift system, which allows the driver to use the gearbox manually or leave the shift work to the automatic transmission. The shift speed can be adapted by selecting one of the settings: manual, comfort, and sport. The body, including doors and bonnet, is constructed out of carbon fiber, delivering the ideal rigidity and strength while

Produced	2003-2010
Engine Size	5439cc
Cylinders	8
0-60 mph	3.6 secs
Top Speed	207.5mph
Power Output	626bhp
Transmission	Automatic
Gears	5 speed
Length	183.3in (4655mm)
Width	75.1in (1908mm)
Height	49.6in (1261mm)
Weight	3898lb (1768kg)
Wheelbase	106.3in (2700mm)

(Specifications refer to 2003 Mercedes-Benz SLR McLaren)

also being lightweight.

The SLR features an electro-hydraulic braking system called Sensotronic Brake Control (SBC), which continuously processes data received from travel and pressure sensors. From this information it calculates the desired brake pressures on the individual wheels. Coupled with the Electronic Stability Program (ESP), the SLR is kept safely on track through brake impulses and a reduction of engine torque when necessary.

The SLR uses carbon ceramic brakes, which demonstrate an extremely high temperature resistance of up to 2192° Fahrenheit (1200° Celsius) – this translates to better stopping power and fade resistance when braking at high speed.

The SLR utilizes active aerodynamics to enhance performance; the adaptive spoiler mounted at the rear works as an airbrake. If great force is applied to the brake pedal, the rear spoiler rises at an angle to create greater aerodynamic drag and consequently boosts the braking effect.

The Roadster variant was released in 2007, sharing the same supercharged V8 engine used in the coupe.

Nissan GT-R

Produced	2007 to date
Engine Size	3799cc
Cylinders	6
0-60 mph	3.5 secs
Top Speed	193mph
Power Output	485bhp
Transmission	Semi-automatic
Gears	6 speed
Length	183.3in (4655mm)
Width	74.6in (1895mm)
Height	53.9in (1370mm)
Weight	3836lb (1740kg)
Wheelbase	109.4in (2780mm)

(Specifications refer to 2007
Nissan GT-R)

The Nissan GT-R (nicknamed "Godzilla" and commonly known as the R35) was originally developed and designed as part of the Skyline series; however, it soon became its very own production model. The GT-R was first introduced at the 2007 Tokyo Motor Show as a two-door front-engined sports car with a lot to offer. Designed by Shirō Nakamura, the GT-R was developed with a distinctive Japanese aesthetic in mind, although the car's final body shape was conceived by American, European, and Japanese designers as a means of fulfilling the demands of a worldwide market.

The GT-R is currently the only vehicle built on Nissan's Premium Midship Platform, which is an evolutionary development of the Front Midship Platform that was featured in the 2001 Skyline series. The GT-R's hybrid unibody assembly consists of a carbon-composite crossmember to stiffen the steel chassis, with aluminum paneling for the doors, hood, and trunk lid. The overall finish of the supercar has been complemented with Nissan's very own uniquely developed paint job – consisting of a six-stage paint process, including a scratch-resistant clear coat and metallic sheen.

While being recognized as the world's first independent transaxle four-wheel drive (a technology that was developed uniquely by Nissan), it's no wonder that the GT-R effectively replaced its reigning predecessor, the Nissan Skyline. Nissan boasted that the 3.8-liter VR38DETT V6 engine and parallel IHI (Ishikawajima-Harima Heavy Industries) twin-turbochargers kicked out an astounding 485bhp and torque rating of 434lb/ft. The supercharged technology beneath the hood meant that the vehicle was recorded with a top speed of 193mph and a 0-60 in 3.5 seconds. The six-speed dual clutch semi-automatic transmission, coupled with the Advanced Total Traction Engineering System for All-terrain (ATTESA), provided power to all four wheels of the GT-R. The Nissan vehicle dynamics control system also aided the stability of the vehicle, even at high speeds.

Since its official 2007 unveiling, the GT-R has undergone several modifications and upgrades in both the production and racing versions; with the GT-R, GT-R SpecV, Super GT (Motorsport vehicle), FIA GT/GT1 World Championship, R35 GT-R Nismo GT1, and R35 GT-R Nismo GT3. With over 6,000 units of the production version having been sold, Nissan have proven that their leaps into developing new technology have a true place in the automotive market.

Noble M600

The Noble M600 is a British hand-built supercar that boasts an impressive power to weight ratio. The ethos behind the car's design was simple: to focus on the more analog qualities of design, unlike many other supercars that boast computer-generated support.

The suspension of the M600 features independent double wishbones with coil over shock absorbers and front and rear roll bars. The stainless steel and aluminum tube has an integral safety cell and rear crash structure, while the carbon fiber composite body makes it extremely light.

Powered by a mid-mounted Yamaha V8 4439 twin-turbo engine, the M600 generates between 450-650bhp depending on settings. It features an Adaptive Performance Control (APC) that enables the driver to select specific power output, traction control, and throttle response according to the location and driving conditions. The APC has three modes: road, track, or race. The road setting represents 450bhp with full traction control, and is used for everyday driving. The track mode offers a sportier ride – pushing the power output up to 550bhp while utilizing a less

Produced	2010 to present
Engine Size	4439cc
Cylinders	8
0-60 mph	3 secs
Top Speed	225mph
Power Output	650bhp
Transmission	Manual
Gears	6 Speed
Length	172in (4360mm)
Width	75in (1910mm)
Height	45in (1140mm)
Weight	2646lb (1200kg)
Wheelbase	100in (2540mm)

(Specifications refer to 2010 Noble M600)

intrusive level traction control and more initial response to throttle. The race mode, as anticipated, boosts the power output to the top end: the V8 generating a massive 650bhp while traction control is reduced to allow increased wheel slip.

The M600 experienced extensive wind tunnel testing to fine-tune the precise design of the body. Every element of its shape is a reflection of the data gathered during the testing phase – its aerodynamic styling maximized for performance and cooling efficiency.

The brakes were developed specially for the M600 in partnership with Alcon, featuring semi-floating front disc and cast aluminum alloy monobloc calipers, while the wheels were exclusively designed for the M600 and manufactured by Speedline in Italy.

Although the M600 has been designed with speed and handling as the initial goal, comfort and practicality have not been diminished in any way; the interior is available in leather or Alcantara and fine quality wool carpets are bound to edges with leather. The carbon fiber seats are designed exclusively for the M600 and can be upholstered according to the client's individual specification.

Prices for the Noble M600 start at $450,000, although right-hand drive is considerably more.

Pagani Zonda

Produced	1999-2011
Engine Size	7291cc
Cylinders	12
0-60 mph	3.5 secs
Top Speed	215mph
Power Output	594bhp
Transmission	Manual
Gears	6 speed
Length	174.6in (4435mm)
Width	80.9in (2055mm)
Height	44.9in (1141mm)
Weight	2809lb (1274kg)
Wheelbase	107.5in (2730mm)

(Specifications refer to 2005 Pagani Zonda F)

The Pagani Zonda made its first public appearance at the 1999 Geneva Motor Show and has been subject to numerous changes during its production. Pagani boasts extensive knowledge of construction using carbon fiber, and the unveiling of the Zonda demonstrated their superb level of craftsmanship with the material, resulting in a top-spec supercar.

The Zonda C12 is the original model; powered by a 6.0-liter Mercedes-Benz V12 engine and coupled with five-speed transmission, it was capable of achieving 0-60 in 4.2 seconds. Just five examples of this variant were produced before the C12-S arrived in 2002. Power was increased with the addition of the larger V12 engine, which had a displacement of 7291cc, pushing the power output up to 547bhp and torque of 550lb/ft. In order to harness the power to the full, traction control and ABS became standard. The overall result was an improvement in handling and performance; the 0-60 sprint was achieved in 3.6 seconds and a top speed of 220mph.

In 2005 Pagani released a re-engineered version named the Zonda F (or Zonda Fangio), in honor of the Formula One champion Juan Manuel Fangio who had been involved in the early development of the Zonda. At the time of its release it was one of the fastest supercars ever built, and Fangio was a great source of inspiration, fueling the company to challenge more established names in the industry such as Ferrari and Lamborghini. The Zonda F shares the 7.3-liter V12 engine with its predecessor but enhanced air intake manifolds enable the car to generate 594bhp and torque of 560lb/ft at 4000rpm, enabling a slightly improved 0-60 performance of 3.5 seconds and a top speed of 215mph.

The carbon fiber bodywork was revised to incorporate a new rear spoiler, and increased vents improved the car's aerodynamics.

The optional packages for the Zonda F featured magnesium wheels to provide better heat conduction while also being lighter, and carbon ceramic brakes developed with Brembo. One year later the Zonda Roadster F debuted at the 2006 Geneva Motor Show. It shared many of the coupe's specifications but featured a removable carbon fiber roof. Using race-derived technology, materials, and construction methods Pagani were able to maintain chassis rigidity without dramatically increasing the overall weight of the car.

Pagani produced 25 examples of the Zonda F and 25 examples of the Roadster variant.

Porsche 911 GT3

The 911 is without doubt one of automotive history's most iconic cars and remains the flagship vehicle in the current line-up at Porsche. During its extensive production years, the 911 has continuously evolved to maximize its power, performance, and reputation. The Porsche 911 GT3 was created in 1999 to provide a platform for the company's productive clubsport division, while also offering a street-legal vehicle. Compared to its predecessor in the 911 series, it boasts increased power, faster performance, and refined styling.

Powered by a 3.6-liter flat-six engine the GT3 has a power output of 435bhp and 317lb/ft of torque – a significant improvement from its predecessor that enables it to boast a 0-60 performance of 4.1 seconds. The Porsche Stability Management (PSM) offers the

Produced	1999 to present
Engine Size	3797cc
Cylinders	6
0-60 mph	4.1 secs
Top Speed	194mph
Power Output	435bhp
Transmission	Manual
Gears	6 speed
Length	175.5in (4460mm)
Width	71.1in (1808mm)
Height	50.3in (1280mm)
Weight	3075lb (1395kg)
Wheelbase	92.7in (2355mm)

(Specifications refer to 2009 Porsche 911 GT3)

option to deactivate the stability control and traction control at the touch of a button, giving unrestricted control over driving dynamics. The aerodynamic styling

increases downforce to both the front and rear of the car, and better grip and stability at high speeds is evident in this model in comparison to earlier 911s. In order to match the increased driving dynamics and performance, Porsche have equipped the GT3 with revised brakes that feature a larger friction disc and aluminum cover to reduce weight. As with all models in the Porsche line-up, the GT3 has experienced numerous evolutionary changes since its inception in 1999.

The latest GT3 features direct fuel injection (DFI) that contributes to engine efficiency as well as power output, which has been increased to 475bhp. It sprints from 0-60 in just 3.5 seconds and has a maximum speed of 196mph. Cosmetically, the

GT3 has been on the receiving end of some modifications, including sizeable air ducts in the new front bumper, vertical air ducts in the rear bumper, and a large wing mounted at the rear with a ram air intake for the rear-mounted engine. The new GT3 also features the latest Porsche Doppelkupplung (PDK) transmission that enables the driver to change gear in milliseconds without interrupting the flow of power, resulting in faster and smoother acceleration.

The Porsche 911 GT3 has enjoyed a successful racing career, regularly winning championship and endurance races including first overall in the 24 Hours Nürburgring six times, and seven victories in the GT class of the American Le Mans Series. It has also proved triumphant in the national Porsche Carrera Cup series and the international Porsche Supercup.

Porsche 918 Spyder

Unveiled at the 2010 80th anniversary Geneva Motor Show, although production didn't begin until three years later, the Porsche 918 Spyder is a limited edition mid-engined plug-in hybrid sports car that has been designed by Michael Mauer. Porsche announced its intention to produce just 918 units of the road version of the 918, which is able to boast some incredible specifications.

The 918 produces 940lb/ft of torque with its 4.6-litre V8, and offers mind-blowing acceleration,

Produced	2013 to present
Engine Size	4593cc
Cylinders	8
0-60 mph	2.6 secs
Top Speed	214mph
Power Output	887bhp
Transmission	Dual-clutch
Gears	7 speed
Length	182.7in (4643mm)
Width	76.3in (1940mm)
Height	45.9in (1167mm)
Weight	3747.8lb (1700kg)
Wheelbase	107.4in (2730mm)

(Specifications refer to 2013 Porsche 918 Spyder)

achieving its 0-60 performance in just 2.6 seconds, and can power on to a top speed of 214mph. It is the first series production car to break the seven-minute barrier at the Nürburgring circuit, achieving an incredible six minutes 57 seconds lap time.

A carbon fiber reinforced plastic monocoque is a contributing factor to the vehicle's aerodynamic performance. It blends tradition with innovation and truly marks a turning point for the company through the use of an exclusively

designed V8 engine, PDK transmission, ceramic composite brakes, and top-mounted exhaust pipes deriving from racetrack models. The total power output of the 918 is an impressive 887bhp, which combines the power of the engine (608bhp) and two electrical motors that directly drive the front and rear axles (154bhp rear and 125bhp front). The energy storage battery is a liquid-cooled lithium-ion battery that utilizes regenerative braking as a charging feature alongside the plug-in charging port. Engineers have also developed active aerodynamics (PAA) to reduce drag and increase downforce through the use of the three-stage extendable rear-wing and active cooling air-flaps in the front air intakes. The supercar offers a variation of different driving modes: E-drive (when the car runs purely from electrical battery power) and three hybrid modes (hybrid, sport, and race). In E-drive mode, the car uses only the electronic motors that power the front and rear axles and can power the car for a range of up to 18 miles, with a top speed of 93mph.

In the cockpit a multifunction steering wheel reinforces the motorsport principles that a driver's hands should never leave the steering wheel, while the center console offers fast navigation to air conditioning, car settings, and the Porsche Communication Management (for personal device connectivity) – all on a gesture-recognition touch screen surface.

The 918 Spyder is more economical and has lower emissions than a Toyota Prius, marking it as an important car within the automotive history. Porsche have harnessed hybrid technology to secure their future with high-spec performance vehicles.

Porsche Carrera GT

The Carrera GT is a high-performance, mid-engined sports car that made its debut in the automotive market in 2004. The GT was originally designed as a racing vehicle (a Le Mans prototype in 1999) that had earlier been put on hold, while the company focused their engineering and marketing efforts on the forthcoming Cayenne SUV model, which was being developed in partnership with Audi and Volkswagen. Upon the grand unveiling, Porsche boasted of a road legal V10 supercar that posed great competition to its direct opposition.

The Carrera GT demonstrated an incredible 605bhp, a top speed of 205mph, and a 0-60 in just 3.9 seconds. Its aerodynamic design featured large side inlets that allowed air to cool the powerful V10 and the automatically deployed rear wing (when the vehicle reaches a speed of 70mph), which had previously been used in many of the 911 series designs. The 68 V10 engine was a design originally built behind closed doors by Porsche for the Footwork Formula One team back in 1992, but was quickly shelved and later resurrected in 1999 for the concept model of the car.

The construction of the bodywork was heavily designed around a carbon fiber monocoque and subframe, including the carbon fiber-framed boot space that housed the V10. The impressive V10 engine meant that the GT required a radiator system that was almost five times the size of that as featured in a 911 Turbo. Porsche had fitted the Carrera with its newest invention: a carbon fiber-reinforced silicon

Produced	2004-2007
Engine Size	5733cc
Cylinders	10
0-60 mph	3.9 secs
Top Speed	205mph
Power Output	605bhp
Transmission	Manual
Gears	6 speed
Length	181.6in (4613mm)
Width	75.6in (1921mm)
Height	45.9in (1166mm)
Weight	3042lb (1380kg)
Wheelbase	107.4in (2730mm)

(Specifications refer to 2004 Porsche Carrera GT)

carbide ceramic composite braking system that gave an even further impressive aesthetic to the already head-turning bodywork of the vehicle. As standard, the Carrera GT was fitted with a Bose audio sound system, onboard navigation system, and a Beechwood-topped gear-knob that paid homage to the original gear stick as featured in the early 917 Le Mans racing vehicles.

Sports Car International voted the Carrera GT number one in its Top Sports Cars of the 2000s, and later voted it number eight in the Top Sports Cars of All Time. Porsche had initially intended on the production total of 1,500 units of the Carrera GT, however due to a change in airbag legislations in the United States they discontinued the model as they approached the manufacture of almost 1,300 vehicles.

SSC Aero

The SSC (formerly known as Shelby Super Cars) Aero is a mid-engined two-door coupe sports car with a lot to brag about. The Aero is a futuristically designed vehicle with body contouring that most car fanatics would only have dreamed of prior to its release. It was in 2004 that the original model of the Aero went into development, based on a replica chassis of a Lamborghini Diablo, with a Corvette C5R engine and a six-speed transmission that was similar to that seen in the Dodge Viper.

Officially launched in 2006, the Ultimate Aero was the final modified production version of the series that again had a lot to boast about. The Shelby Super Cars Ultimate Aero (twin-turbo edition) was the world's fastest

Produced	2006-2013
Engine Size	6340cc
Cylinders	8
0-60 mph	2.78 secs
Top Speed	257mph
Power Output	1287bhp
Transmission	Manual
Gears	6 speed
Length	176.2in (4475mm)
Width	82.7in (2101mm)
Height	43in (1092mm)
Weight	2750lb (1247kg)
Wheelbase	105.2in (2672mm)

(Specifications refer to 2006 SSC Ultimate Aero)

production car for a three-year period between 2007-2010, where it was heralded in the *Guinness Book of Records* until the Bugatti Veyron Super Sport knocked the Aero off pole position. With its aerodynamic shaping, lightweight engine, and supercharged boost capabilities, the Aero is renowned as one of the fastest road legal supercars ever built. With a ground clearance of just four inches, the Ultimate Aero was designed for a single purpose: driving at incredible speed on the open road.

The supercar features many jaw-dropping attributes, which all stem from the original design of the Aero developed by Jerod Shelby. The supercharged V8 Chevrolet 6.34-liter engine was tweaked to produce an astounding 1287bhp, with a torque rating of 1112lb/ft – one of the fastest production-designed engines of its time. The car was constructed using a carbon fiber composite and steel spaceframe that made the vehicle light on the ground; this incredible feat of engineering saw the Ultimate Aero produce a spectacular top speed of 257mph and a 0-60 in just 2.78 seconds. To add to its existing aesthetic value the car was fitted with vertical doors (also known as butterfly doors) and on the inside the standard fittings were also of a notable quality; a CD/DVD system with a 7.5" display was accompanied by a 10-speaker audio system, alongside all of the expected accessories.

This car really was built with the "true driving experience" in mind, as it was not fitted with electronic assistant aids such as ABS or traction control. After a seven-year reign, the SSC Ultimate Aero finally had its production ceased in 2013 as SSC made way for its ultimate new offering: the Tuatara.